Hello, 이솝우화!

개정판

③

Hello, 이솝우화! 3 (개정판)

2007년 6월 19일 초판 1쇄 펴냄
2023년 10월 20일 개정판 1쇄 펴냄

원작 이솝
글 국제어학연구소 영어학부편
감수 이동호
그림 조한유·유지환·서은정
펴낸이 이규인
펴낸곳 국제어학연구소 출판부
출판등록 2010년 1월 18일 제302-2010-000006호
주소 서울특별시 마포구 대흥로4길 49, 1층(용강동 월명빌딩)
Tel (02) 704-0900 **팩시밀리** (02) 703-5117
홈페이지 www.bookcamp.co.kr
e-mail changbook1@hanmail.net

ISBN 979-11-9792044-8 (13740)
정가 16,800원

영어의 기초를 다져 주는

magic

Hello, 이솝우화!

개정판

③

원작 이솝 ┃ 글 국제어학연구소 영어학부
감수 이동호 ┃ 그림 조한유·유지환·서은정

ILR 국제어학연구소

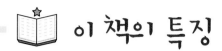

이 책의 특징

    이 책은 아이들에게 친숙한 이솝우화를 영어로 읽으면서, 자연스럽게 영어의 낱말과 표현을 학습하게 하는 책입니다. '이제 막 영어를 배우기 시작한 아이들이 영어문장을 이해할 수 있을까?' 라고 생각할 수도 있을 것입니다. 하지만 이솝우화는 거의 모든 아이들이 이미 알고 있는 이야기입니다. 또한 예쁜 그림으로 설명이 뒷받침되기 때문에, 스토리에 나오는 낱말과 표현을 쉽고도 재미있게 이해할 수 있습니다.

    이 책은 또한 언어의 습득 과정인 듣기 → 말하기 → 읽기 → 쓰기의 순서대로 학습이 진행됩니다. 이렇게 다양한 방법으로 여러 번 낱말과 표현을 익히게 되면, 쉽게 잊어버리지 않으므로 진정한 자기의 실력이 됩니다.

    이 책의 목적은 스토리에 나오는 모든 낱말과 표현을 이해하는 것이 아닙니다. 스토리에 나오는 낱말과 표현 중에서도 중요한 낱말과 표현만을 골라 학습하게 합니다.

    낱말 익히기와 표현 익히기에서 배우게 되는 낱말과 표현만 알아도 상당한 효과를 얻을 수 있습니다. 그러면서도 스토리를 통해서 영어를 익히게 되므로, 기본적인 문장 감각을 몸에 베이게 하는 효과를 볼 수 있습니다.

 부모님! 이렇게 지도해 주세요!

➊ 예비학습

스토리 이후의 학습에서 본격적인 학습이 이루어지므로, 예비학습은 그림을 한 번 보고, 듣는 정도로 가볍게 넘기세요.

➋ 스토리

스토리의 낱말과 문장을 모두 이해하려고 하지 마세요. 낱말과 표현 익히기에서 배우게 되는 낱말과 표현만 확실히 알게 해주셔도 아주 좋은 효과를 얻을 수 있습니다.

❸ 낱말 익히기와 표현 익히기

스토리에서 나온 낱말과 표현을 익히는 과정입니다. 먼저 MP3를 들으면서 따라 말하고, 따라 씁니다. 이 단계에서는 낱말과 표현을 확실하게 익히는 것이 좋으므로, 필요하다면 MP3를 다시 들으면서 다른 노트에 더 써보는 것도 좋은 방법입니다.

이렇게 확실하게 익힌 후에 문제를 풀게 되는데, 듣기 → 말하기 → 읽기 → 쓰기의 순서로 문제를 풀게 되므로, 보다 쉽고 확실하게 낱말과 표현을 확인할 수 있습니다.

❹ 뽀너스! 뽀너스!

사자(lion)와 쥐(mouse)를 영어로 배우면, 호기심 많은 아이들은 '그럼 다른 동물들은 영어로 뭐라고 할까? 라는 의문이 생기겠죠? 또 '나는 너무 졸려(I'm too sleepy.)' 라는 표현을 배우면, 그럼 '나는 너무 피곤해.' 는 영어로 뭐라고 할까? 라는 의문도 생길 것입니다.

이 단계는 이러한 궁금점을 해소함과 동시에 같은 범주에 있는 새로운 낱말과 표현을 확장해서 배우게 되는 효과가 있습니다.

❺ Dictation

Dictation은 우리말로 '받아쓰기' 라는 말이에요. 이 교재에서는 단순히 영어 낱말이나 표현을 듣고 받아쓰는 것이 아니라, 앞에서 배웠던 스토리를 그림과 함께 보여주면서, 문장의 빈칸을 채워서 쓰도록 합니다. 따라서 스토리에 대한 이해를 함께 할 수 있습니다.

원어민이 천천히 읽기는 하지만, 한 문장 한 문장을 놓치지 않고 집중해야 빈칸에 알맞은 낱말이나 표현을 쓸 수 있습니다. 만일 놓쳤다해도 MP3를 다시 들으면서 끝까지 모두 쓰도록 하세요.

❻ 스토리 이해하기

이제까지의 학습으로 중요 영어 낱말과 표현, 또한 스토리의 내용을 이해하게 되었을 것입니다. 이 단계는 이제까지 학습한 내용을 문장을 통해서 확인해보는 단계입니다.

앞에서 배운 내용보다는 난이도가 있지만, 이제까지 충실하게 교재를 학습했다면 충분히 풀 수 있는 문제들이므로, 자신감을 가지고 도전하세요!

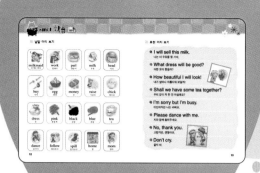

예비학습

스토리를 읽기 전에, 스토리에 나오는
낱말과 표현을 미리 익혀요.

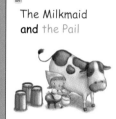

스토리

원어민의 정확한 발음으로 스토리를
들으면서 어떤 내용인지 파악해요.

낱말 익히기와 표현 익히기

원어민의 발음을 그대로 따라 하고, 읽고, 쓰면서
낱말과 표현을 익혀요.

듣기, 말하기, 읽기, 쓰기 문제

앞에서 익힌 낱말과 표현을
듣기 → 말하기 → 읽기 → 쓰기의
순서대로 문제를 풀어요.

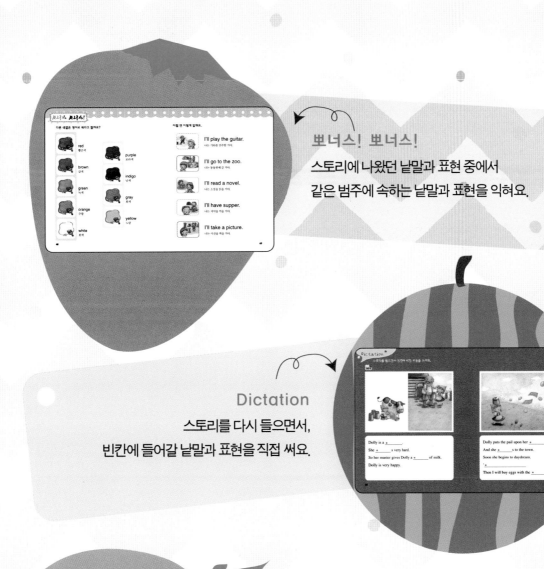

뽀너스! 뽀너스!

스토리에 나왔던 낱말과 표현 중에서
같은 범주에 속하는 낱말과 표현을 익혀요.

Dictation

스토리를 다시 들으면서,
빈칸에 들어갈 낱말과 표현을 직접 써요.

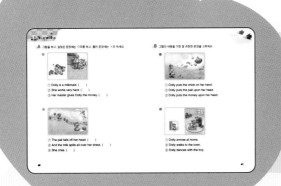

스 토 리 이해하기

그림과 문장을 통해서 배운 스토리를
잘 이해하고 있는지 확인해요.

차 례

The Milkmaid and the Pail · 10

The Hare and the Tortoise · 64

The Farmer and the the Golden Egg · 118

우리말 해석과 정답

이런 뜻이에요!

예비 학습   듣기   말하기   읽기   쓰기

The Milkmaid
and the Pail

예비 학습 MP3

❊ 낱말 미리 보기

milkmaid
젖 짜는 여자

work
일하다

pail
양동이

milk
우유

head
머리

buy
사다

egg
달걀

money
돈

raise
기르다

chick
병아리

dress
옷

pink
분홍색

black
검정

blue
파랑

tea
차

dance
춤추다

follow
따라오다

spill
엎지르다

home
집

mom
엄마

- **I will sell this milk.**
  나는 이 우유를 팔 거야.

- **What dress will be good?**
  어떤 옷이 좋을까?

- **How beautiful I will look!**
  내가 얼마나 아름다워 보일까!

- **Shall we have some tea together?**
  우리 같이 차 한 잔 하실래요?

- **I'm sorry but I'm busy.**
  미안하지만 나는 바빠요.

- **Please dance with me.**
  저와 함께 춤춰주세요.

- **No, thank you.**
  고맙지만, 괜찮아요.

- **Don't cry.**
  울지 마.

The Milkmaid and the Pail

Dolly is a **milkmaid**.

She **work**s very hard.

So her master gives Dolly

a **pail** of **milk**.

Dolly is very happy.

Dolly puts the **pail** upon her **head**.

And she walks to the town.

Soon she begins to daydream.

'I will **sell this milk**.

Then I will **buy eggs** with the **money**.'

16

Dolly keeps daydreaming.

'I will **raise** lots of **chick**s.

Then I will sell the chickens.

Then I will **buy** a new **dress**.'

'What dress will be good?

A **pink dress**?

No, **pink** is too bright for me.

A **black dress**?

No, **black** is too dark.'

'A **blue dress**?

Yes, that will be good.

The color **blue** looks nice on me.

OK. I will **buy** a **blue dress**.

How beautiful I will look!'

'Boys will come and speak to me.

"Shall we have some tea together?"

Then I will say, "I'm sorry but I'm busy."

And I won't care about them.'

'I will go to a party.

Then boys will ask me,

"Shall we **dance** together?"

And I will say, "No, thank you."

'Then boys will **follow** me.

"Please dance with me."

But I will pass them

with a toss of my **head**.'

Then she tosses her **head** for practice.

Just then,

the **pail** falls off her **head**.

And the **milk spills** all over.

She cries and says.

"My **milk**, my **money**, my **dress!**"

She arrives at **home**.

Mom says, "What happened?"

She tells her **mom** the truth.

"Don't cry.

It's no use crying over **spilled milk**."

낱말을 듣고, 따라 말하고, 따라 써보세요.

milkmaid [mílkmèid] 젖 짜는 여자

milkmaid _____ _____

work [wə:rk] 일하다

work _____ _____

pail [peil] 양동이

pail _____ _____

milk [milk] 우유

milk _____ _____

head [hed] 머리

head _____ _____

34

buy [bai] 사다

buy _____ _____ _____

egg [eg] 달걀

egg _____ _____ _____

money [mʌ́ni] 돈

money _____ _____ _____

raise [reiz] 기르다

raise _____ _____ _____

chick [tʃik] 병아리

chick _____ _____ _____

dress [dres] 옷

dress _____ _____

pink [piŋk] 분홍색

pink _____ _____

black [blæk] 검정

black _____ _____

blue [bluː] 파랑

blue _____ _____

tea [tiː] 차

tea _____ _____

dance [dæns] 춤추다

dance

follow [fálou] 따라오다

follow

spill [spil] 엎지르다

spill

home [houm] 집

home

mom [mɑm] 엄마

mom

들려주는 낱말이 그림과 어울리면 ○표, 어울리지 않으면 ×표를 하세요.

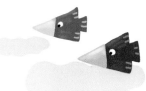

그림에 알맞은 낱말을 보기에서 골라 말해보세요.

mom, pink, black, head, milk, pail, chick

그림을 보고 올바른 철자에 동그라미하세요.

1

he ed
ad

2

w or k
al

3

spi ll
ek

4

t ea
p

5

ra iz e
is

6

bl ack
vl

7

m il k
ir

8

bl un
ue

낱말의 철자를 순서대로 바르게 나열하세요.

① 옷 　　esdrs 　　_____　　⑪ 양동이 　　aipl 　　_____

② 머리 　　edha 　　_____　　⑫ 병아리 　　ickhc 　　_____

③ 집 　　ohem 　　_____　　⑬ 젖짜는 여자 　　aimkidlm 　　_____

④ 돈 　　nmyeo 　　_____　　⑭ 따라오다 　　wolflo 　　_____

⑤ 일하다 　　okwr 　　_____　　⑮ 달걀 　　geg 　　_____

⑥ 기르다 　　ireas 　　_____　　⑯ 차 　　aet 　　_____

⑦ 분홍색 　　nikp 　　_____　　⑰ 춤추다 　　cdena 　　_____

⑧ 파랑 　　ebul 　　_____　　⑱ 엄마 　　omm 　　_____

⑨ 사다 　　uyb 　　_____　　⑲ 검정 　　kbcla 　　_____

⑩ 우유 　　lmki 　　_____　　⑳ 엎지르다 　　lislp 　　_____

표현 익히기 표현을 듣고, 따라 말하고, 따라 쓰세요.

● **I will sell this milk.** 나는 이 우유를 팔 거야.

    I will sell this milk.

● **What dress will be good?** 어떤 옷이 좋을까?

    What dress will be good?

● **How beautiful I will look!**
내가 얼마나 아름다워 보일까!

    How beautiful I will look!

● **Shall we have some tea together?** 같이 차 한 잔 하실래요?

    Shall we have some tea together?

● **I'm sorry but I'm busy.** 미안하지만 나는 바빠요.

    I'm sorry but I'm busy.

● **Please dance with me.** 저와 함께 춤춰주세요.

Please dance with me.

_____

● **No, thank you.** 고맙지만, 괜찮아요.

No, thank you.

_____

● **Don't cry.** 울지 마.

Don't cry.

_____

'우리 ~ 할까요?'의 표현

상대방에게 '우리 ~ 할까요?'라고 표현할 때는 Shall we~? 를 써요.
문장 뒤에 together를 붙이면 '같이'하자는 뜻이 더 잘 전달된답니다.

- Shall we **have some tea together?**   우리 같이 차 한 잔 할까요?
- Shall we **dance together?**   우리 같이 춤출까요?
- Shall we **play basketball?**   우리 농구할래?
- Shall we **sing a song?**   우리 노래 부를래?

그림을 보고, 알맞은 표현을 고르세요.

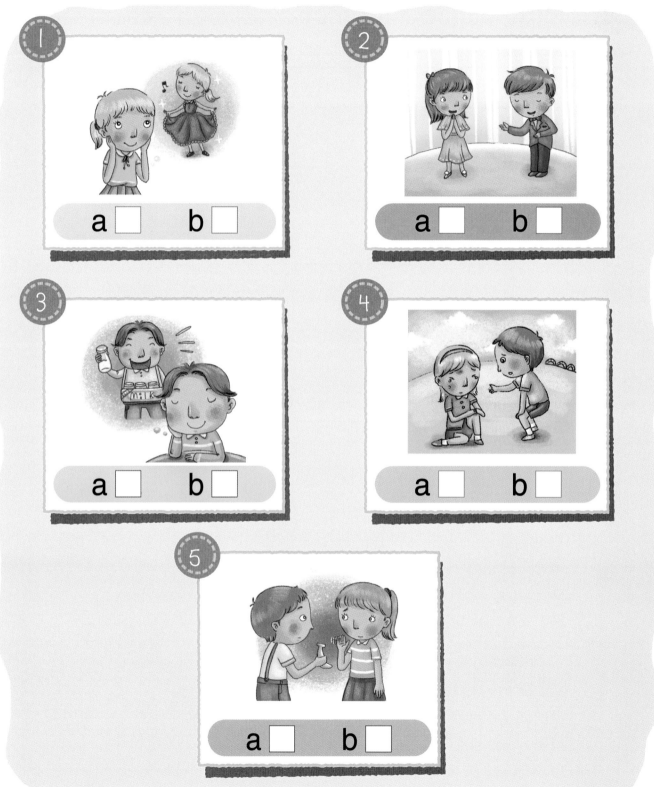

1 a ☐   b ☐

2 a ☐   b ☐

3 a ☐   b ☐

4 a ☐   b ☐

5 a ☐   b ☐

그림에 알맞은 표현을 보기에서 골라 말해보세요.

Please dance with me.   What dress will be good?
No, thank you.   How beautiful I will look!

①

②

③

④

그림과 문장이 서로 어울리도록 알맞은 낱말을 골라 동그라미 하세요.

①  What dress will be bad ?
(good)

②  No, thank you.
Yes

③  I will sell this milk .
chick

④  How angry I will look!
beautiful

⑤ Don't cry .
say

우리말에 맞는 낱말 카드를 골라 동그라미하고, 빈칸에 순서대로 쓰세요.

① 저와 함께 춤춰주세요.

Please   have   dance   with   you   me .

➜ _____

② 나는 이 우유를 팔 거야.

I'm   I will   sell   buy   this milk .

➜ _____

③ 같이 차 한 잔 하실래요?

Shall we   with   have some   tea   egg   together ?

➜ _____

④ 어떤 옷이 좋을까?

What dress   is   will be   look   good ?

➜ _____

다른 색깔은 영어로 뭐라고 할까요?

red
빨간색

purple
보라색

brown
갈색

indigo
남색

green
녹색

gray
회색

orange
주황

yellow
노랑

white
흰색

이럴 땐 이렇게 말해요.

I'll play the guitar.

나는 기타를 연주할 거야.

I'll go to the zoo.

나는 동물원에 갈 거야.

I'll read a novel.

나는 소설을 읽을 거야.

I'll have supper.

나는 저녁을 먹을 거야.

I'll take a picture.

나는 사진을 찍을 거야.

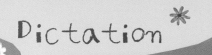
스토리를 들으면서 빈칸에 빠진 부분을 쓰세요.

Dolly is a ❶ _____ .

She ❷ _____ s very hard.

So her master gives Dolly a ❸ _____ of milk.

Dolly is very happy.

Dolly puts the pail upon her ④_____.

And she ⑤_____s to the town.

Soon she begins to daydream.

'⑥_____

Then I will buy eggs with the ⑦_____.'

Dolly keeps daydreaming.

'I will ❶ _____ lots of ❷ _____ s.

Then I will sell the chickens.

Then I will ❸ _____ a new dress.'

'④_____

A ⑤ _____ dress?

No, pink is too bright for me.

A ⑥ _____ dress?

No, black is too dark.'

'A ① _____ dress?

Yes, that will be good.

The color blue looks nice on me.

OK. I will buy a blue ② _____.

③ _____ ,

'Boys will come and speak to me.

"④_____ have some tea together?"

Then I will say, "⑤_____."

And I won't care about them.'

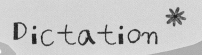

'I will go to a party.

Then ① _____s will ask me,

"Shall we ② _____ together?"

And I will say, "③ _____."

'Then boys will ④ _____ me.

" ⑤ _____ "

But I will pass them with a toss of my head.'

Then she tosses her head for practice.

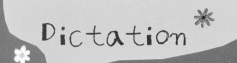

Just then, the pail falls off her head.

And the milk ① _____s all over.

She cries and says.

"My ② _____, my money, my ③ _____"

She arrives at ④_____.

Mom says, "What happened?"

She tells her ⑤_____ the truth.

"⑥_____.

It's no use crying over spilled milk."

A 그림을 보고, 알맞은 문장에는 ○표를 하고, 틀린 문장에는 ✕표 하세요.

①

① Dolly is a milkmaid. (   )

② She works very hard. (   )

③ Her master gives Dolly the money. (   )

②

① The pail falls off her head. (   )

② And the milk spills all over her dress. (   )

③ She cries. (   )

B 그림의 내용을 가장 잘 표현한 문장을 고르세요.

① Dolly puts the chick on her hand.

② Dolly puts the pail upon her head.

③ Dolly puts the money upon her head.

① Dolly arrives at home.

② Dolly walks to the town.

③ Dolly dances with the boy.

그림의 내용을 보고, 빈칸에 알맞은 낱말을 보기에서 골라 쓰세요.

보기 **black, tea, dress, dark, come, busy, pink**

①

'Boys will ❶_____ and speak to me.

"Shall we have some ❷_____ together?"

Then I will say, "I'm sorry but I'm ❸_____."

②

'What ❶_____ will be good?

A ❷_____ dress? No, pink is too bright for me.

A ❸_____ dress?

No, black is too ❹_____.'

D 주어진 표현을 이용하여 그림의 내용에 맞도록 문장을 쓰세요.

①

그는 학교에 걸어서 가요.
(school / he / walks / to)

➜ _____

②

나는 모자를 살 거예요.
(a cap / I / buy / will)

➜ _____

③

우리는 매우 열심히 공부해요.
(very / we / study / hard)

➜ _____

④

그는 매우 화를 내요.
(angry / he / very / is)

➜ _____

이런 뜻이에요!

 예비학습

 듣기

 말하기

 읽기

 쓰기

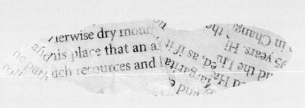

The Hare and the Tortoise

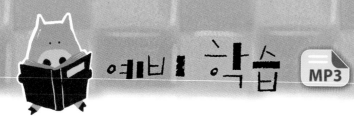

🌸 낱말 미리 보기

hare
토끼

fast
빠른

tortoise
거북

slow
느린

angry
화난

race
경주

top
꼭대기

hill
언덕

gather
모이다

frog
개구리

behind
~뒤에

nap
낮잠

think
생각하다

tired
피곤한

wake
잠이 깨다

line
선

yell
외치다

snail
달팽이

late
늦은

win
이기다

※ 표현 미리 보기

● **I am the fastest animal in the woods.**
나는 숲에서 가장 빠른 동물이야.

● **How slowly you walk!**
너는 어쩜 그렇게 느리게 걷니!

● **Can't you walk a little faster?**
좀 더 빨리 걸을 수 없니?

● **Let's race to the top of the hill.**
언덕 꼭대기까지 경주하자!

● **Ready, steady, go!**
제자리에, 준비, 출발!

● **I will take a nap here.**
여기에서 낮잠을 잘 거야.

● **You can do it!**
너는 해낼 수 있어.

● **Hurry up!**
서둘러!

The Hare and the Tortoise

The **hare** can run very **fast**.

She is proud of herself about it.

The **hare** says,

"I am the fastest animal

in the woods."

One day, the **hare** meets a **tortoise**.

"How slowly you walk!

Can't you walk a little faster?"

says the **hare**.

"Yes, I'm **slow**, but I'm steady,"
says the **tortoise**.

"Steady is not important," says the **hare**.

The **tortoise** is **angry**.

"Steady is important! I'll prove it.

How about a **race**?" says the **tortoise**.

"A **race**! You and me?" laughs the **hare**.

"No problem," says the **hare**.

"Let's race to the top of the hill.

I'll beat you easy-peasy."

Many animals **gather** around them.

The **frog** says, "Ready, steady, go!"

The **hare** and the **tortoise** start.

The **hare** runs as **fast** as the wind.

But the **tortoise** walks very slowly.

GO

Soon the **hare** runs away.

She looks **behind** her.

But she can't see the **tortoise**.

She says, "I will take a nap here."

And the **hare** sleeps under the tree.

Meanwhile, the **tortoise** goes slowly.

He sees the **hare** is sleeping.

He **think**s, 'She must be tired.

Better not to **wake** her.'

And he keeps on walking.

The **tortoise** comes closer to the finish **line**.

Animals shout loudly.

"You can do it!

Hurry up, **tortoise**," **yells** the **snail**.

The **tortoise** keeps on walking.

Just then, the **hare wake**s up.

And then she remembers the **race**.

So she runs as **fast** as she can.

But it's too **late**.

The **tortoise** reaches the finish **line**.

The **tortoise** says,

"**Slow** and steady **wins** the **race**."

낱말 익히기

낱말을 듣고, 따라 말하고, 따라 써보세요.

hare [hɛər] 토끼

hare _____ _____

fast [fǽst] 빠른

fast _____ _____

tortoise [tɔ́ːrtəs] 거북

tortoise _____ _____

slow [slou] 느린

slow _____ _____

angry [ǽŋgri] 화난

angry _____ _____

race [reis] 경주

race _____ _____ _____

top [tap] 꼭대기

top _____ _____ _____

hill [hil] 언덕

hill _____ _____ _____

gather [gǽðər] 모이다

gather _____ _____ _____

frog [frɔːg] 개구리

frog _____ _____ _____

behind [biháind] ~ 뒤에

behind _____ _____ _____

nap [næp] 낮잠

nap _____ _____ _____

think [θiŋk] 생각하다

think _____ _____ _____

tired [taiərd] 피곤한

tired _____ _____ _____

wake [weik] 잠이 깨다

wake _____ _____ _____

line [lain] 선

line

yell [jel] 외치다

Yell

snail [sneil] 달팽이

Snail

late [leit] 늦은

late

win [win] 이기다

win

들려주는 낱말에 맞는 그림을 골라 동그라미하세요.

①

②

③

④

⑤

⑥

그림에 알맞은 낱말을 보기에서 골라 말해보세요.

hare, tortoise, snail, angry, nap, frog

그림을 보고 올바른 철자에 동그라미하세요.

1.  ra se / ce

2.  t ir / ar ed

3.  h ac / ar e

4.  an / en gry

5.  di / be hind

6.  lat e / y

7.  f / p ast

8.  ter / tor toise

가로와 세로 열쇠를 보고, 낱말 퍼즐을 풀어보세요.

가로열쇠 ② 모이다 ⑤ 빠른 ⑨ ~뒤에 ⑩ 언덕 ⑬ 거북 ⑮ 이기다 ⑯ 외치다 ⑲ 꼭대기 ⑳ 잠이 깨다

세로열쇠 ❶ 개구리 ❸ 경주 ❹ 토끼 ❻ 화난 ❼ 선 ❽ 느린 ⑪ 피곤한 ⑫ 달팽이 ⑭ 생각하다 ⑰ 늦은 ⑱ 낮잠

① f

② g   ③ r

④ h

⑤ f

⑥ a   ⑦ l   ⑧ s

⑨ b   ⑩ h

⑪ t   ⑫ s

⑬ t   ⑮ w

⑭ t

⑯ y   ⑰ l   ⑱ n

⑲ t

⑳ w

표현 익히기 표현을 듣고, 따라 말하고, 따라 쓰세요.

● **I am the fastest animal in the woods.**
나는 숲에서 가장 빠른 동물이야.

I am the fastest animal in the woods.

_____

● **How slowly you walk!** 너는 어쩜 그렇게 느리게 걷니!

How slowly you walk!

_____

● **Can't you walk a little faster?** 좀 더 빨리 걸을 수 없니?

Can't you walk a little faster?

_____

● **Let's race to the top of the hill.** 언덕 꼭대기까지 경주하자!

Let's race to the top of the hill.

_____

● **Ready, steady, go!** 제자리에, 준비, 출발!

Ready, steady, go!

_____

96

I will take a nap here. 여기에서 낮잠을 잘 거야.

I will take a nap here.

You can do it! 너는 해낼 수 있어.

You can do it!

Hurry up! 서둘러!

Hurry up!

제안의 표현

상대방에게 '우리 ~하자'라고 제안할 때는 동사 앞에 let's를 써서 표현해요. let's는 let us를 줄여서 쓰는 말이에요.

- Let's race to the top of the hill. 언덕 꼭대기까지 경주하자!
- Let's have lunch together. 점심 같이 먹자.
- Let's buy tickets. 티켓을 사자.
- Let's go by subway. 지하철 타고 가자.

들려주는 표현이 어울리는 그림을 골라 순서대로 번호를 쓰세요.

그림에 알맞은 표현을 보기에서 골라 말해보세요.

 보기

Ready, steady, go!   Let's race to the top of the hill.
Hurry up!   I will take a nap here.

①

②

③

④

그림과 문장이 서로 어울리도록 연결하세요.

1.  • • I will take a nap here.

2.  • • Hurry up!

3.  • • Let's race to the top of the hill.

4.  • • Ready, steady, go!

5.  • • You can do it!

우리말 표현을 보고, 밑줄 친 부분에 들어갈 낱말을 골라 쓰세요.

1 좀 더 빨리 걸을 수 없니?

→ Can't you walk a little _____?

☐ slower
☐ faster

2 너는 어쩜 그렇게 느리게 걷니!

→ How slowly you _____ now!

☐ gather
☐ walk

3 나는 숲에서 가장 빠른 동물이야.

→ I am the fastest _____ in the woods.

☐ animal
☐ frog

4 여기에서 낮잠을 잘 거야.

→ I will take a _____ here.

☐ nap
☐ win

5 언덕 꼭대기까지 경주하자!

→ Let's race to the top of the _____.

☐ late
☐ hill

101

쁘너스 쁘너스!

다른 신체 부위의 이름은 뭐라고 할까요?

hip
엉덩이

knee
무릎

elbow
팔꿈치

toe
발가락

neck
목

back
등

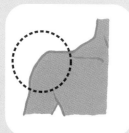

shoulder
어깨

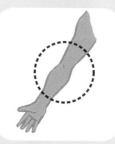

arm
팔

hand
손

finger
손가락

이럴 땐 이렇게 말해요.

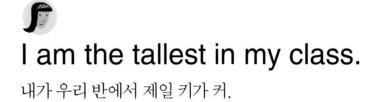

I am the tallest in my class.
내가 우리 반에서 제일 키가 커.

I am the strongest.
내가 가장 힘이 세.

I am the funniest in the club.
내가 클럽에서 제일 웃겨.

I am the prettiest.
내가 제일 예뻐.

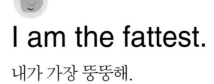

I am the fattest.
내가 가장 뚱뚱해.

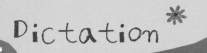

스토리를 들으면서 빈칸에 빠진 부분을 쓰세요.

The hare can run very ❶_____.

She is proud of herself about it.

The ❷_____ says,

"❸_____ in the woods."

One day, the hare meets a tortoise.

" ④ _____

Can't you ⑤ _____ a little faster?" says the hare.

"Yes, I'm ⑥ _____, but I'm steady,"

says the tortoise.

"Steady is not important," says the hare.

The tortoise is ❶_____.

"Steady is important! I'll prove it.

How about a ❷_____?" says the tortoise.

"A race! You and me?" ❸_____s the hare.

"No problem" ④_____s the hare.

"⑤_____ of the hill.

I'll beat you easy-peasy."

Many animals ❶_____ around them.

The frog says, " ❷_____ ."

The hare and the tortoise start.

The hare runs as ❸_____ as the wind.

But the tortoise walks very slowly.

Soon the hare runs away.

She looks ④_____ her.

But she can't see the tortoise.

She says, "⑤_____."

And the hare sleeps under the tree.

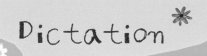

Meanwhile, the ① _____ goes slowly.

He sees the hare is sleeping.

He ② _____ s, 'She must be tired.

Better not to ③ _____ her.'

And he keeps on walking.

The tortoise comes closer to the finish ④_____.

Animals shout loudly.

" ⑤_____

Hurry up, tortoise," yells the ⑥_____.

The tortoise keeps on walking.

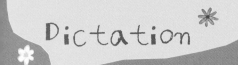

Just then, the hare ① _____ s up.

And then she remembers the ② _____ .

So she runs as ③ _____ as she can.

But it's too ④_____.

The tortoise reaches the finish line.

The tortoise says,

"Slow and steady ⑤_____s the race."

A 그림을 보고, 알맞은 문장에는 ◯표를 하고, 틀린 문장에는 ✕표 하세요.

1

① Many animals gather around them. (   )

② The frog says, "I will take a nap here." (   )

③ The hare and the snail start. (   )

2

① The tortoise comes closer to the finish line. (   )

② The hare shouts loudly. (   )

③ The tortoise keeps on walking. (   )

B 그림의 내용을 가장 잘 표현한 문장을 고르세요.

①

① The tortoise is angry.

② The tortoise is happy.

③ The tortoise walks slowly.

②

① The snail sleeps under the tree.

② The hare sleeps under the tree.

③ The tortoise sleeps behind the tree.

C 그림의 내용을 보고, 빈칸에 알맞은 낱말을 보기에서 골라 쓰세요.

tired, top, think, hill, wake, sleep

①

He sees the hare is ❶_____ing.

The tortoise ❷_____s, "She must be ❸_____.

Better not to ❹_____ her."

And he keeps on walking.

②

"No problem," says the hare.

"Let's race to the ❶_____ of the ❷_____.

I'll beat you easy-peasy."

D 주어진 표현을 이용하여 그림의 내용에 맞도록 문장을 쓰세요.

그는 계속 공부해요.
(keeps on / studying / he)

➡ _____

우리는 크게 소리 질러요.
(shout / we / loudly)

➡ _____

③

나는 그녀가 춤추는 걸 봐요.
(I / dancing / see / her)

➡ _____

④

그녀는 바이올린을 켤 수 있어.
(can / the violin / she / play)

➡ _____

이런 뜻이에요!

예비 학습　듣기　말하기　읽기　쓰기

The Farmer and the Golden Egg

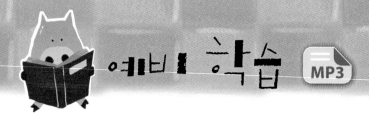

낱말 미리 보기

young
젊은

farmer
농부

greedy
욕심 많은

rich
부유한

morning
아침

breakfast
아침식사

goose
거위

cage
우리

surprised
놀란

shine
빛나다

luck
행운

dream
꿈

happy
행복한

clean
청소하다

kiss
입맞추다

love
사랑하다

hit
치다

knee
무릎

kill
죽이다

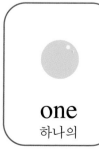

one
하나의

120

● **I want to get rich quickly.**
나는 빨리 부자가 되고 싶어.

● **I'll eat eggs for breakfast.**
아침식사로 계란을 먹어야겠다.

● **This is a golden egg!**
이것은 황금알이야.

● **I am rich now.**
나는 이제 부자다.

● **I love you so much.**
나는 널 너무 사랑해.

● **I'm getting rich.**
나는 부자가 되고 있어.

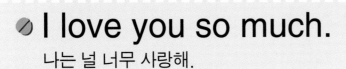

● **I'll kill my goose.**
나는 거위를 죽일 거야.

● **I won't be rich anymore.**
나는 더 이상 부자가 될 수 없어.

The Farmer and the Golden Egg

There is a **young farmer**.

He is a **greedy** man.

He thinks, 'I want to get rich quickly.'

One **morning,** he gets up early.

He says, "I'm hungry.

I'll eat eggs for breakfast."

So he goes out to get some eggs.

He goes to his **goose**'s **cage**.

And he takes out an egg.

He sees the egg.

And he is very **surprised**.

It is gold and **shining**

in the sun.

"This is a golden egg!" the **young farmer** shouts. "I am rich now." The **young farmer** cannot believe his **luck**. His **dream** is coming true.

Every day his **goose** lays

a golden egg.

And every day he becomes richer.

He is very **happy**.

He gives his **goose** good food.

And he **clean**s her **cage**

every day.

He **kiss**es her and says,

"I love you so much."

But the **young farmer** is **greedy**.

He thinks, 'I'm getting rich.

But I'm not getting **rich** quickly.

How can I get **rich** more quickly?'

The **young farmer hits** his **knee**.

"I know what I'll do.

I'll kill my goose," he says.

"There must be many golden eggs

inside her."

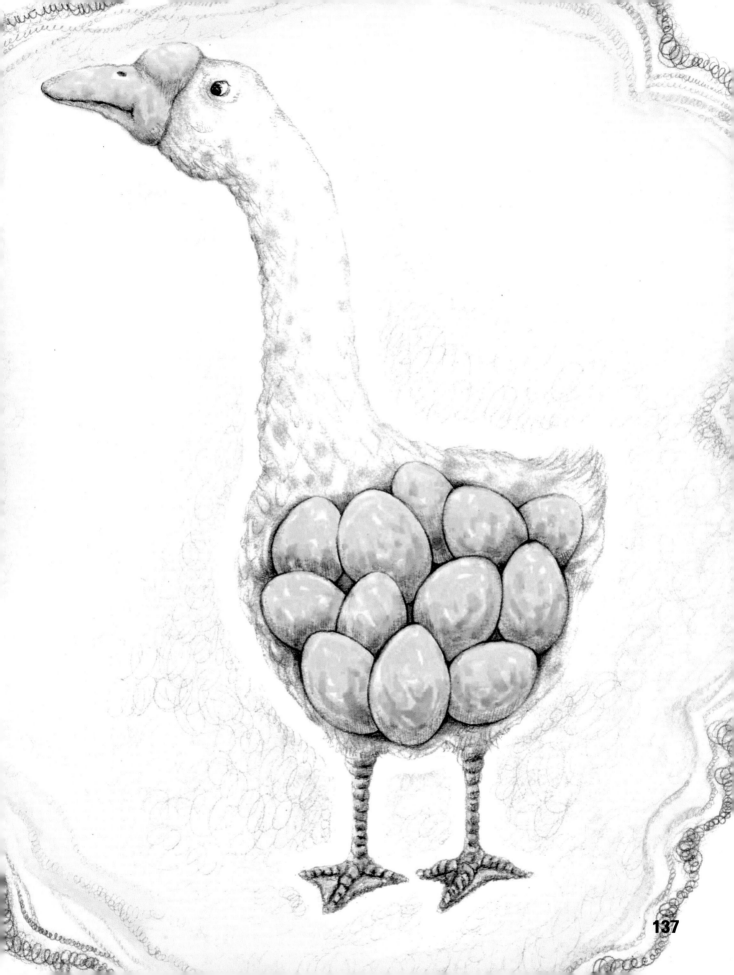

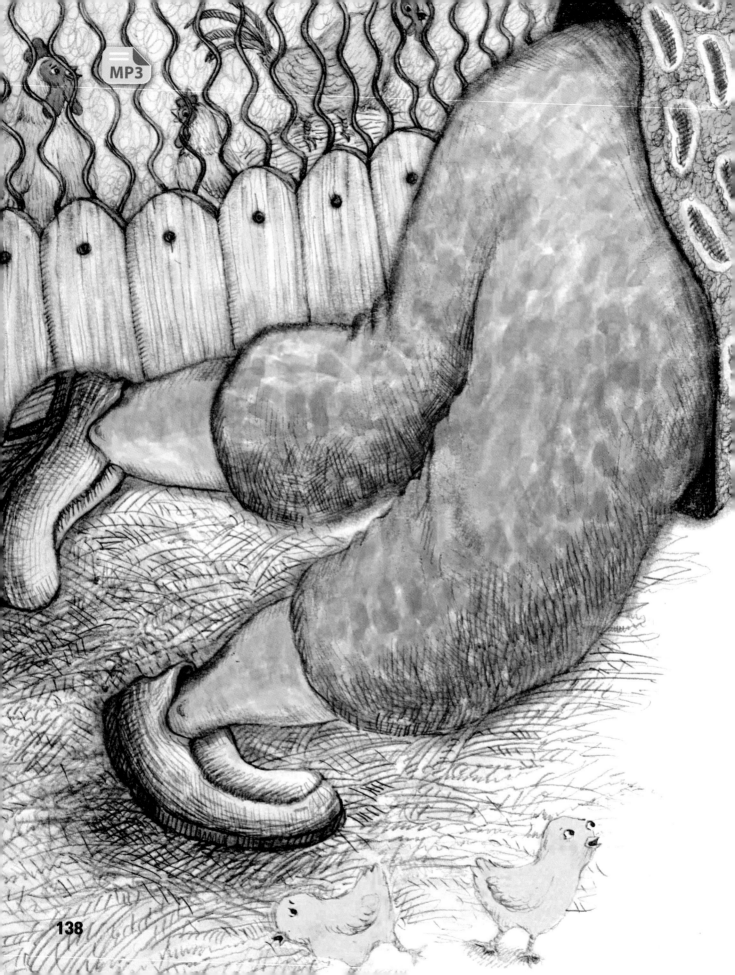

So he takes his
goose and **kill**s her.
And what happens?
There isn't **one** golden egg inside her.

He cries,

"Now the **goose** is dead.

So she won't lay any more

golden eggs.

I won't be rich anymore."

He regrets **kill**ing the **goose**.

낱말을 듣고, 따라 말하고, 따라 써보세요.

young [jʌŋ] 젊은

young _____ _____

farmer [fɑːrmər] 농부

farmer _____ _____

greedy [gríːdi] 욕심 많은

greedy _____ _____

rich [ritʃ] 부유한

rich _____ _____

morning [mɔ́ːrniŋ] 아침

morning _____ _____

breakfast [brékfəst] 아침식사

breakfast   _____   _____

goose [guːs] 거위

goose   _____   _____

cage [keidʒ] 우리

cage   _____   _____

surprised [sərpráizd] 놀란

surprised   _____   _____

shine [ʃain] 빛나다

shine   _____   _____

luck [lʌk] 행운

luck _____ _____

dream [driːm] 꿈

dream _____ _____

happy [hǽpi] 행복한

happy _____ _____

clean [kliːn] 청소하다

clean _____ _____

kiss [kis] 입맞추다

kiss _____ _____

love [lʌv] 사랑하다

love _____ _____ _____

hit [hit] 치다

hit _____ _____ _____

knee [niː] 무릎

knee _____ _____ _____

kill [kil] 죽이다

kill _____ _____ _____

one [wʌn] 하나의

one _____ _____ _____

그림을 보고, 들려주는 낱말 중에서 알맞은 것을 고르세요.

그림에 알맞은 낱말을 보기에서 골라 말해보세요.

rich, dream, kiss, goose, knee, cage

1

2

3

4

5

6

필요하지 않은 알파벳에 ×표 하고, 그림에 해당하는 낱말을 쓰세요.

1. goo×se

goose

2. richf

3. yluck

4. fajrmer

5. happty

6. onue

7. cglean

8. knvee

9. xyoung

연결된 낱말 띠에서 우리말에 해당하는 낱말을 찾아 동그라미하고,
우리말 옆에 다시 쓰세요.

nphc**morning**apvzkissyuxzkneetujqonebx

① 아침   *morning*

② 입맞추다 _____

③ 무릎 _____

④ 하나의 _____

bqlovekyhjcbreakfastmfghitcptsurpriseda

⑤ 사랑하다 _____

⑥ 아침식사 _____

⑦ 치다 _____

⑧ 놀란 _____

cvbecleanalkyrichxzwqdreamopsjluckfrth

⑨ 청소하다 _____

⑩ 부유한 _____

⑪ 꿈 _____

⑫ 행운 _____

ftwleygooseewqogreedyjkuhappytufarmer

⑬ 거위 _____

⑭ 욕심 많은 _____

⑮ 행복한 _____

⑯ 농부 _____

xrqcagedreopjeshinesqtkillbnmyoungvczl

⑰ 우리 _____

⑱ 빛나다 _____

⑲ 죽이다 _____

⑳ 젊은 _____

표현 익히기　　표현을 듣고, 따라 말하고, 따라 쓰세요.

● **I want to get rich quickly.**
나는 빨리 부자가 되고 싶어.

I want to get rich quickly.

_____

● **I'll eat eggs for breakfast.**
아침식사로 계란을 먹어야지.

I'll eat eggs for breakfast.

_____

● **This is a golden egg!** 이것은 황금알이

This is a golden egg!

_____

● **I am rich now.** 나는 이제 부자다.

I am rich now.

_____

● **I love you so much.** 나는 널 너무 사랑해.

I love you so much.

_____

I'm getting rich. 나는 부자가 되고 있어.

I'm getting rich.

I'll kill my goose. 나는 거위를 죽일 거야.

I'll kill my goose.

I won't be rich anymore.

나는 더 이상 부자가 될 수 없어.

I won't be rich anymore.

✳ **this와 that의 표현**

어떤 것을 지시해서 말할 때 '이것', '저것'이라고 말을 하죠? 이 말을 영어로 this와 that이라고 말해요. 가까이 있는 것을 가리킬 때는 this를 쓰고, 멀리 있는 것을 가리킬 때는 that을 써요.

• This is a golden egg!	이것은 황금 알이다!
• This is my umbrella.	이것은 내 우산이다.
• That is a red cap.	저것은 빨간 모자이다.
• That is my bag.	저것은 내 가방이다.

들려주는 표현 중에서 어울리는 그림을 골라 (a) 또는 (b)를 쓰세요.

그림에 알맞은 표현을 보기에서 골라 말해보세요.

I am rich now.	I'll eat eggs for breakfast.
I'll kill my goose.	I won't be rich anymore.

1

2

그림과 문장이 서로 어울리도록 알맞은 낱말을 골라 동그라미하세요.

1

I ⟨love⟩ you so much.
hate

2

I'll kill my goose.
kiss

3

This is a silver egg.
golden

4

I am rich now.
young

5

I'll eat apples for breakfast.
eggs

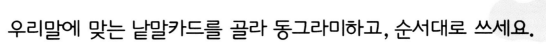

우리말에 맞는 낱말카드를 골라 동그라미하고, 순서대로 쓰세요.

① 나는 부자가 되고 있어.

I'm   I won't   getting   rich .

→ _____

② 아침식사로 계란을 먹어야겠다.

I'll   eat eggs   eat goose   for   breakfast .

→ _____

③ 나는 더 이상 부자가 될 수 없어.

I won't   be greedy   be rich   anymore .

→ _____

④ 나는 거위를 죽일 거야.

I'll   kill   my mouse   my goose .

→ _____

뽀너스 뽀너스!

다른 직업은 뭐라고 할까요?

artist
화가

baker
제빵사

singer
가수

writer
작가

reporter
기자

teacher
선생님

doctor
의사

nurse
간호사

fire fighter
소방수

police officer
경찰

이럴 땐 이렇게 말해요.

I want to be pretty.
나는 예뻐지고 싶어.

I want to be young.
나는 젊어지고 싶어.

I want to be strong.
나는 강해지고 싶어.

I want to be slim.
나는 날씬해지고 싶어.

I want to be tall.
나는 키 크고 싶어.

I want to win the race.
나는 경기에서 이기고 싶어.

There is a ① _____ farmer.

He is a ② _____ man.

He thinks, 'I want to get ③ _____ quickly.'

One ④ _____, he gets up early.

He says, "I'm ⑤ _____.

⑥ _____"

So he goes out to get some eggs.

Dictation

He goes to his goose's ① _____ .

And he takes out an egg.

He sees the egg.

And he is very ② _____ .

It is gold and ③ _____ing in the sun.

"_____"
    ④
the young farmer shouts.

"_____"
    ⑤
The young farmer cannot believe his ⑥ _____.

His ⑦ _____ is coming true.

Every day his ❶ _____ lays a golden egg.

And every day he becomes richer.

He is very ❷ _____ .

He gives his goose good food.

And he ③ _____s her cage every day.

He ④ _____es her and says,

"⑤ _____"

But the young ❶_____ is greedy.

He thinks, '❷_____.

But I'm not getting rich quickly.

How ❸_____ I get rich more quickly?'

164

The young farmer hits his ④_____.

"I know what I'll do.

⑤_____ ", he says.

"There must be many golden eggs inside her."

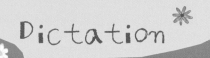

So he takes his ❶ _____ and kills her.

And what happens?

There isn't ❷ _____ golden egg inside her.

166

He cries, "Now the goose is dead.

So she won't lay any more golden ③_____s.

④_____."

He regrets killing the goose.

A 그림을 보고, 알맞은 문장에는 ○표를 하고, 틀린 문장에는 ✕표 하세요.

① He goes to the hill. (　　)

② He takes out an egg. (　　)

③ It is gold and shining in the sun. (　　)

① He gives his dog good food. (　　)

② He cleans her cage every day. (　　)

③ He hits his goose. (　　)

B 그림의 내용을 가장 잘 표현한 문장을 고르세요.

1

① One morning, he sleeps late.

② One morning, he gets up early.

③ One morning, he goes to the woods.

2

① He takes his goose and kills her.

② He takes his mouse and kills her.

③ He takes his goose and kisses her.

C 그림의 내용을 보고, 빈칸에 알맞은 내용을 보기에서 골라 쓰세요.

> 보기   **egg, luck, kill, rich, dream, goose**

①

He cries, "Now the ❶ _____ is dead.
So she won't lay any more golden ❷ _____s.
He regrets ❸ _____ing the goose.

②

"I am ❶ _____ now."
The young farmer cannot believe his ❷ _____.
His ❸ _____ is coming true.

D 주어진 표현을 이용하여 그림의 내용에 맞도록 문장을 쓰세요.

①

우리는 부엌을 청소해요.
(clean / we / the kitchen)

➜ _____

②

나는 그녀에게 곰인형을 줘요.
(give / a teddy bear / her / I)

➜ _____

③

그는 매우 놀라요.
(surprised / he / very / is)

➜ _____

④

그녀는 돈을 꺼내요.
(she / some money / takes out)

➜ _____

The Milkmaid and the Pail

⟨14p-15p⟩

Dolly is a milkmaid.
She works very hard.
So her master gives Dolly a pail of milk.
Dolly is very happy.

돌리는 젖 짜는 소녀예요.
그녀는 매우 열심히 일해요.
그래서 주인이 돌리에게 우유 한 통을 줘요.
돌리는 매우 행복해요.

⟨16p-17p⟩

Dolly puts the pail upon her head.
And she walks to the town.
Soon she begins to daydream.
'I will sell this milk.
Then I will buy eggs with the money.'

돌리는 머리 위에 통을 올려요.
그리고 그녀는 마을로 걸어가요.
곧 그녀는 상상을 하기 시작해요.
'나는 이 우유를 팔 거야.
그런 다음에 그 돈으로 달걀을 사야지.'

⟨18p-19p⟩

Dolly keeps daydreaming.
'I will raise lots of chicks.
Then I will sell the chickens.
Then I will buy a new dress.'

돌리는 계속 상상을 해요.
'나는 병아리를 많이 기를 거야.
그러고 나서 닭을 팔아야지.
그 다음에 나는 새 옷을 살 거야.'

⟨20p-21p⟩

'What dress will be good?
A pink dress?
No, pink is too bright for me.
A black dress?
No, black is too dark.'

'무슨 옷이 좋을까?
분홍색 드레스?
아니야, 분홍색은 나한테 너무 밝아.
검은색 드레스?
아니야, 검은색은 너무 어두워.'

⟨22p-23p⟩

'A blue dress?
Yes, that will be good.
The color blue looks nice on me.
OK. I will buy a blue dress.
How beautiful I will look!'

'파란색 드레스?
그래, 그것이 좋겠어.
파란색은 나와 잘 어울리지.
좋아. 파란색 드레스를 살 거야.
내가 얼마나 아름다워 보일까!'

〈24p-25p〉

'Boys will come and speak to me.
"Shall we have some tea together?"
Then I will say, "I'm sorry but I'm busy."
And I won't care about them.'

'소년들이 나에게 와서 말을 걸겠지.
"우리 같이 차 한 잔 할까요?"
그러면 나는 말할 거야, "미안하지만 저는 바쁘답니다."
그러면서 나는 그들에게 관심을 보이지 않을 거야.'

〈26p-27p〉

'I will go to a party.
Then boys will ask me,
"Shall we dance together?"
And I will say, "No, thank you."

'난 파티에 갈 거야.
그러면 소년들이 나에게 묻겠지.
"우리 함께 춤출까요?"
그러면 나는 말할 거야, "감사하지만, 사양하겠어요."

〈28p-29p〉

'Then boys will follow me.
"Please dance with me."
But I will pass them with a toss of my head.'
Then she tosses her head for practice.

'그러면 소년들이 나를 따라올 거야.
"저와 함께 춤춰주세요."
그러나 나는 머리를 새침하게 들면서 지나가 버려야지.'
그러면서 그녀는 진짜로 머리를 새침하게 들어요.

〈30p-31p〉

Just then, the pail falls off her head.
And the milk spills all over.
She cries and says.
"My milk, my money, my dress!"

바로 그때, 통이 머리에서 떨어져요.
그리고 우유가 모두 쏟아져요.
그녀는 울면서 말해요.
"내 우유, 내 돈, 내 드레스."

〈32p-33p〉

She arrives at home.
Mom says, "What happened?"
She tells her mom the truth.
"Don't cry.
It's no use crying over spilled milk."

소녀가 집에 도착해요.
엄마가 말해요, "무슨 일이니?"
소녀는 모든 사실을 말해요.
"울지 마,
엎질러진 우유를 두고 울어봤자 소용없어."

낱말 익히기

🎧 듣기 문제 ·················· 38p

(듣기대본)
① pail ② egg ③ head
④ black ⑤ work ⑥ money
⑦ dance ⑧ dress ⑨ milk

정답 ••••••••••••••••••

① ○ ② ○ ③ ×
④ × ⑤ × ⑥ ○
⑦ ○ ⑧ × ⑨ ○

🐭 말하기 문제 ·················· 39p

① milk ② mom ③ head
④ chick ⑤ pink ⑥ black ⑦ pail

🐱 읽기 문제 ·················· 40p

① ad ② or ③ ll
④ t ⑤ is ⑥ bl
⑦ il ⑧ ue

✏️ 쓰기 문제 ·················· 41p

① dress ② head
③ home ④ money
⑤ work ⑥ raise
⑦ pink ⑧ blue
⑨ buy ⑩ milk

⑪ pail ⑫ chick
⑬ milkmaid ⑭ follow
⑮ egg ⑯ tea
⑰ dance ⑱ mom
⑲ black ⑳ spill

표현 익히기

🐶 듣기 문제 ·················· 44p

(듣기대본)
①(a) How beautiful I will look!
　(b) I'm sorry but I'm busy.

②(a) Please dance with me.
　(b) Shall we have some tea together?

③(a) I will sell this milk.
　(b) No, thank you.

④(a) What dress will be good?
　(b) Don't cry.

⑤(a) I'm sorry but I'm busy.
　(b) No, thank you.

정답 ••••••••••••••••••

① (a) ② (a) ③ (a) ④ (b) ⑤ (b)

말하기 문제 ·················· 45p

❶ What dress will be good?
❷ No, thank you.
❸ Please dance with me.
❹ How beautiful I will look!

읽기 문제 ·················· 46p

❶ good
❷ No
❸ milk
❹ beautiful
❺ cry

쓰기 문제 ·················· 47p

❶ Please dance with me.
❷ I will sell this milk.
❸ Shall we have some tea together?
❹ What dress will be good?

Dictation

50p-51p

❶ milkmaid ❷ work ❸ pail ❹ head
❺ walk   ❻ I will sell this milk.
❼ money

52p-53p

❶ raise ❷ chick ❸ buy

❹ What dress will be good?
❺ pink   ❻ black

54p-55p

❶ blue   ❷ dress
❸ How beautiful I will look!
❹ Shall we
❺ I'm sorry but I'm busy

56p-57p

❶ boy   ❷ dance   ❸ No, thank you
❹ follow   ❺ Please dance with me.

58p-59p

❶ spill   ❷ milk   ❸ dress
❹ home   ❺ mom   ❻ Don't cry.

스토리 이해하기 ·········· 60p-63p

A ❶ ① ○   ② ○   ③ ×
  ❷ ① ○   ② ×   ③ ○

B ❶ ②   ❷ ①

C ❶ ① come ② tea ③ busy
  ❷ ① dress ② pink ③ black
     ④ dark

D ❶ He walks to school.
  ❷ I will buy a cap.
  ❸ We study very hard.
  ❹ He is very angry.

The Hare and the Tortoise

⟨68p-69p⟩

The hare can run very fast.
She is proud of herself about it.
The hare says,
"I am the fastest animal in the woods."

토끼는 매우 빨리 달릴 수 있어요.
토끼는 그것을 자랑스러워해요.
토끼는 말해요.
"나는 숲에서 가장 빠른 동물이야."

⟨70p-71p⟩

One day, the hare meets a tortoise.
"How slowly you walk!
 Can't you walk a little faster?" says the hare.
"Yes, I'm slow, but I'm steady,"
says the tortoise.

어느 날, 토끼는 거북을 만나요.
"너는 어쩌면 그렇게 느리게 걷니!
 좀 더 빨리 걸을 수 없어?" 토끼가 말해요.
"그래, 난 느려, 하지만 꾸준해."
거북은 말해요.

⟨72p-73p⟩

"Steady is not important," says the hare.
The tortoise is angry.
"Steady is important! I'll prove it.
 How about a race?" says the tortoise.
"A race! You and me?" laughs the hare.

"꾸준한 것은 중요하지 않아." 토끼는 말해요.
 거북은 화가 나요.
"꾸준한 것은 중요해! 내가 그걸 증명해 보이겠어.
 경주 한 번 하는 게 어때?" 라고 거북은 말해요.
"경주라고? 너와 내가?" 토끼는 웃어요.

⟨74p-75p⟩

"No problem," says the hare.
"Let's race to the top of the hill.
 I'll beat you easy-peasy."

"문제없어." 라고 토끼가 말해요.
"언덕 꼭대기까지 경주하자.
 너를 아주 쉽게 이길 거야."

⟨76p-77p⟩

Many animals gather around them.
The frog says, "Ready, steady, go!"
The hare and the tortoise start.
The hare runs as fast as the wind.
But the tortoise walks very slowly.

많은 동물들이 그들 주변으로 모여요.
개구리가 말해요. "제자리에, 준비, 출발!"
토끼와 거북이 출발해요.
토끼는 바람처럼 빨리 달려요.
그러나 거북은 너무 느리게 걸어요.

⟨78p-79p⟩

Soon the hare runs away.
She looks behind her.
But she can't see the tortoise.
She says, "I will take a nap here."
And the hare sleeps under the tree.

곧 토끼는 멀리 달려가 버려요.
토끼는 뒤를 돌아봐요.
그러나 거북은 보이지 않아요.
토끼는 말해요. "여기에서 낮잠을 자야겠다."
그리고 토끼는 나무 아래에서 잠을 자요.

⟨80p-81p⟩

Meanwhile, the tortoise goes slowly.
He sees the hare is sleeping.
He thinks, 'She must be tired.
Better not to wake her.'
And he keeps on walking.

한편, 거북은 느리게 가고 있어요.
그는 토끼가 자는 걸 보아요.
거북은 생각해요. '토끼는 피곤한 게 틀림없어.
깨우지 않는 것이 좋겠어.'
그리고 거북은 계속 걸어요.

⟨82p-83p⟩

The tortoise comes closer to the finish line.
Animals shout loudly.
"You can do it!
 Hurry up, tortoise," yells the snail.
The tortoise keeps on walking.

거북은 점점 결승선에 가까이 다가가요.
동물들은 크게 소리를 질러요.
"너는 할 수 있어!
 서둘러, 거북아." 달팽이가 외쳐요.
거북은 계속 걸어요.

⟨84p-85p⟩

Just then, the hare wakes up.
And then she remembers the race.
So she runs as fast as she can.

바로 그때, 토끼가 잠에서 깨어나요.
그리고 나서 토끼는 경주를 기억해요.
그래서 최대한 빨리 달려요.

⟨86p-87p⟩

But it's too late.
The tortoise reaches the finish line.
The tortoise says,
"Slow and steady wins the race."

그러나 너무 늦었어요.
거북은 결승선에 도착해요.
거북은 말해요.
"천천히 그리고 꾸준히 하면 경주에서 이긴단다."

듣기 대본 및 정답

낱말 익히기

 듣기 문제 ······················· 92p

(듣기대본)
❶ gather ❷ snail ❸ nap
❹ wake ❺ hill ❻ win

정답

❶ 두번째 그림 ❷ 첫번째 그림 ❸ 첫번째 그림
❹ 두번째 그림 ❺ 첫번째 그림 ❻ 두번째 그림

 말하기 문제 ···················93p

❶ angry ❷ nap ❸ frog
❹ tortoise ❺ hare ❻ snail

 읽기 문제 ······················ 94p

❶ ce ❷ ir ❸ ar
❹ an ❺ be ❻ e
❼ f ❽ tor

✎ 쓰기 문제 ······················ 95p

❶ frog ❷ gather ❸ race
❹ hare ❺ fast ❻ angry
❼ line ❽ slow ❾ behind
❿ hill ⓫ tired ⓬ snail
⓭ tortoise ⓮ think ⓯ win
⓰ yell ⓱ late ⓲ nap
⓳ top ⓴ wake

표현 익히기

 듣기 문제 ······················· 98p

(듣기대본)
❶ You can do it!
❷ I will take a nap here.
❸ Let's race to the top of the hill.
❹ Ready, steady, go!
❺ Hurry up!
❻ I am the fastest animal in the woods.

정답

2, 6
1, 5
4, 3

 말하기 문제 ·····················99p

❶ Let's race to the top of the hill.
❷ Ready, steady, go!
❸ Hurry up!
❹ I will take a nap here.

📖 읽기 문제 ·····················100p

❶ Let's race to the top of the hill.
❷ You can do it!
❸ I will take a nap here.
❹ Hurry up!
❺ Ready, steady, go!

178

쓰기 문제 ························· 101p

① faster ② walk ③ animal
④ nap   ⑤ hill

Dictation

104p-105p

① fast ② hare

③ I am the fastest animal

④ How slowly you walk!

⑤ walk ⑥ slow

106p-107p

① angry ② race ③ laugh ④ say

⑤ Let's race to the top

108p-109p

① gather ② Ready, steady, go!

③ fast   ④ behind

⑤ I will take a nap here.

110p-111p

① tortoise ② think ③ wake

④ line ⑤ You can do it! ⑥ snail

112p-113p

① wake ② race ③ fast

④ late   ⑤ win

스토리 이해하기 ········· 114p-117p

A ① ① ○ ② × ③ ×
  ② ① ○ ② × ③ ○

B ① ① ② ②

C ① ① sleep ② think ③ tired ④ wake
  ② ① top   ② hill

D ① He keeps on studying.
  ② We shout loudly.
  ③ I see her dancing.
  ④ She can play the violin.

The Farmer
and the Golden Egg

〈122p-123p〉

There is a young farmer.
He is a greedy man.
He thinks,'I want to get rich quickly.'

젊은 농부가 있어요.
그는 욕심이 많은 사람이에요.
그는 생각해요. '나는 빨리 부자가 되고 싶어.'

〈124p-125p〉

One morning, he gets up early.
He says, "I'm hungry.
I'll eat eggs for breakfast."
So he goes out to get some eggs.

어느 날 아침, 그는 일찍 일어나요.
그는 말해요, "배가 고프네.
아침식사로 계란을 먹어야지."
그래서 그는 달걀을 꺼내러 가요.

〈126p-127p〉

He goes to his goose's cage.
And he takes out an egg.
He sees the egg.
And he is very surprised.
It is gold and shining in the sun.

그는 거위 우리로 가요.
그리고 그는 알을 꺼내요.
그는 알을 봐요.
그리고 그는 매우 놀라요.
그것은 금이며, 태양 아래에서 빛나요.

〈128p-129p〉

"This is a golden egg!"
 the young farmer shouts.
"I am rich now."
The young farmer cannot believe his luck.
His dream is coming true.

"이건 황금알이야!"
젊은 농부가 소리쳐요.
"나는 이제 부자다."
젊은 농부는 자신의 행운을 믿을 수가 없어요.
그의 꿈이 실현되고 있어요.

〈130p-131p〉

Every day his goose lays a golden egg.
And every day he becomes richer.
He is very happy.

매일 그의 거위는 황금알을 낳아요.
그리고 그 농부는 점점 부자가 돼요.
그는 매우 행복해요.

〈132p-133p〉

He gives his goose good food.
And he cleans her cage every day.
He kisses her and says,
"I love you so much."

그는 거위에게 좋은 음식을 줘요.
그리고 그는 매일 거위의 우리를 청소해요.
그는 거위에게 입 맞추며 말해요.
"나는 너를 너무 사랑해"

〈134p-135p〉

But the young farmer is greedy.
He thinks, 'I'm getting rich.
But I'm not getting rich quickly.
How can I get rich more quickly?'

하지만 젊은 농부는 욕심이 많아요.
그는 생각해요, '나는 부자가 되고 있어.
하지만 빨리 부자가 되지는 않아.
어떻게 해야 더 빨리 부자가 될까?'

〈136p-137p〉

The young farmer hits his knee.
"I know what I'll do.
I'll kill my goose," he says.
"There must be many golden eggs inside
her."

젊은 농부는 무릎을 쳐요.
"내가 뭘 해야 할 지 알았어.
나는 거위를 죽일 거야." 그는 말해요.
"거위 속에는 분명히 황금알이 많이 있을 거야."

〈138p-139p〉

So he takes his goose and kills her.
And what happens?
There isn't one golden egg inside her.

그래서 그는 거위를 잡아서 죽여요.
그런데 무슨 일이 일어날까요?
거위 안에는 단 한 개의 황금알도 없어요.

〈140p-141p〉

He cries, "Now the goose is dead.
So she won't lay any more golden eggs.
I won't be rich anymore."
He regrets killing the goose.

그는 울어요, "이제 거위는 죽었어.
그래서 더 이상 황금알을 낳지 못해.
나는 이제 더 이상 부자가 될 수 없어."
그는 거위를 죽인 것을 후회해요.

낱말 익히기

🐶 듣기 문제 ···················· 146p

(듣기대본)

1 (a) shine   (b) surprised
2 (a) clean   (b) happy
3 (a) luck   (b) cage
4 (a) kill   (b) hit
5 (a) goose   (b) love
6 (a) rich   (b) kiss
7 (a) young   (b) morning
8 (a) knee   (b) greedy
9 (a) dream   (b) one

정답

1 a	2 a	3 b
4 a	5 b	6 b
7 a	8 b	9 a

🐱 말하기 문제 ···················· 147p

1 rich   2 dream   3 cage
4 kiss   5 knee   6 goose

📖 읽기 문제 ···················· 148p

1 goose   2 rich   3 luck
4 farmer   5 happy   6 one
7 clean   8 knee   9 young

🏠 쓰기 문제 ···················· 149p

1 morning   2 kiss   3 knee
4 one   5 love   6 breakfast
7 hit   8 surprised 9 clean
10 rich   11 dream   12 luck
13 goose   14 greedy   15 happy
16 farmer   17 cage   18 shine
19 kill   20 young

표현 익히기

🐶 듣기 문제 ···················· 152p

(듣기대본)

1 (a) I'm hungry.
   (b) I will kill my goose.
2 (a) This is a golden egg.
   (b) I love you so much.
3 (a) I'll eat eggs for breakfast.
   (b) I am rich now.

정답

1 b, a	2 a, b	3 b, a

🐭 말하기 문제 ······················ 153p

❶ I am rich now.
　 I won't be rich anymore.
❷ I'll eat eggs for breakfast.
　 I'll kill my goose.

🐱 읽기 문제 ······················· 154p

❶ love ❷ kill ❸ golden
❹ rich ❺ eggs

🦓 쓰기 문제 ······················· 155p

❶ I'm getting rich.
❷ I'll eat eggs for breakfast.
❸ I won't be rich anymore.
❹ I'll kill my goose.

Dictation

158p-159p

❶ young ❷ greedy ❸ rich
❹ morning ❺ hungry
❻ I'll eat eggs for breakfast.

160p-161p

❶ cage ❷ surprised ❸ shin
❹ This is a golden egg!
❺ I am rich now.
❻ luck ❼ dream

162p-163p

❶ goose ❷ happy ❸ clean
❹ kiss ❺ I love you so much.

164p-165p

❶ farmer ❷ I'm getting rich.
❸ can ❹ knee ❺ I'll kill my goose.

166p-167p

❶ goose ❷ one ❸ egg
❹ I won't be rich anymore.

스토리 이해하기 ········ 168p-171p

A ❶ ① × ② ○ ③ ○
　 ❷ ① × ② ○ ③ ×

B ❶ ② ❷ ①

C ❶ ① goose ② egg ③ kill
　 ❷ ① rich ② luck ③ dream

D ❶ We clean the kitchen.
　 ❷ I give her a teddy bear.
　 ❸ He is very surprised.
　 ❹ She takes out some money.

이솝우화
부족카드

milkmaid

work

pail

milk

head

buy

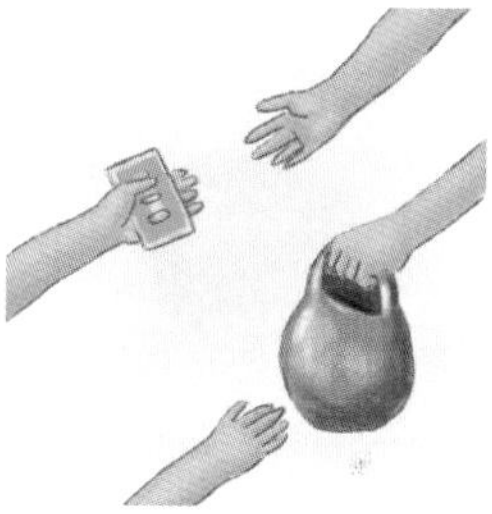

egg

money

raise

chick

일하다

work

젖 짜는 여자

milkmaid

우유

milk

양동이

pail

사다

buy

머리

head

돈

money

달걀

egg

병아리

chick

기르다

raise

dress

pink

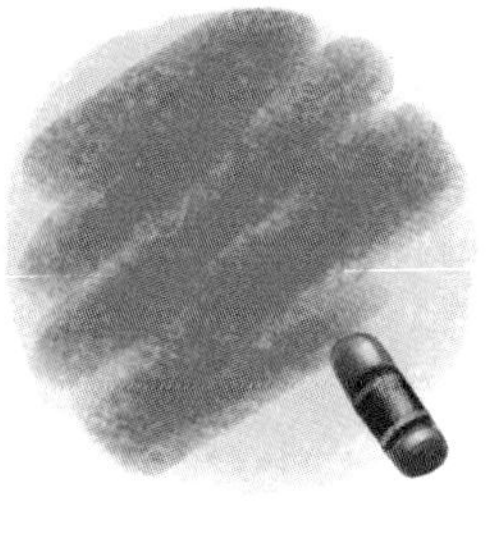

black

blue

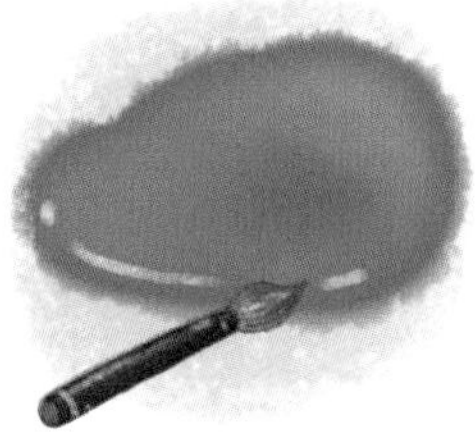

tea

dance

follow

spill

home

mom

분홍색

pink

옷

dress

파랑

blue

검정

black

춤추다

dance

차

tea

엎지르다

spill

따라오다

follow

엄마

mom

집

home

hare

fast

tortoise

slow

angry

race

top

hill

gather

frog

빠른
fast

토끼
hare

느린
slow

거북
tortoise

경주
race

화난
angry

언덕
hill

꼭대기
top

개구리
frog

모이다
gather

behind

nap

think

tired

wake

line

yell

snail

late

win

낮잠

nap

~뒤에

behind

피곤한

tired

생각하다

think

선

line

잠이 깨다

wake

달팽이

snail

외치다

yell

이기다

win

늦은

late

young

farm

greedy

rich

morning

breakfast

goose

cage

surprised

shine

farm
농부

young
젊은

rich
부유한

greedy
욕심 많은

breakfast
아침 식사

morning
아침

cage
우리

goose
거위

shine
빛나다

surprised
놀란

luck

dream

happy

clean

kiss

love

hit

knee

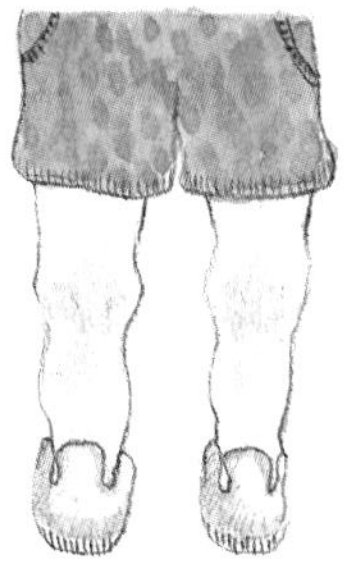

kill

one

꿈
dream

행운
luck

청소하다
clean

행복한
happy

사랑하다
love

입맞추다
kiss

무릎
knee

치다
hit

하나의
one

죽이다
kill

I will sell this milk.

What dress will be good?

How beautiful I will look!

Shall we have some tea together?

I'm sorry but I'm busy.

Please dance with me.

No, thank you.

Don't cry.

I am the fastest animal in the woods.

How slowly you walk!

Can't you walk a little faster?

Let's race to the top of the hill.

어떤 옷이 좋을까?　　난 이 우유를 팔 거야.

우리 같이 차 한 잔 하실래요?　내가 얼마나 아름다워 보일까!

저와 함께 춤춰주세요.　미안하지만 저는 바쁘답니다.

울지 마.　　고맙지만, 괜찮아요.

넌 어쩜 그렇게 느리게 걷니!　나는 숲에서 가장 빠른 동물이야.

언덕 꼭대기까지 경주하자!　좀 더 빨리 걸을 수 없니?

Ready, steady, go!

I will take a nap here.

You can do it!

Hurry up!

I want to get rich quickly.

I'll eat eggs for breakfast.

This is a golden egg!

I am rich now.

I love you so much.

I'm getting rich.

I'll kill my goose.

I won't be rich anymore.

여기에서 낮잠을 잘 거야.　제자리에, 준비, 출발!

서둘러!　　　　넌 해낼 수 있어.

나는 아침식사로 계란을 먹어야지.　나는 빨리 부자가 되고 싶어.

나는 이제 부자다.　이것은 황금 알이다!

나는 부자가 되고 있어.　나는 널 너무 사랑해.

나는 더 이상 부자가 될 수 없어.　나는 거위를 죽일 거야.